NATIONAL
GEOGRAPHIC
KiDS

You Can Be an
Entomologist!

Dino Martins, Ph.D.

NATIONAL GEOGRAPHIC
WASHINGTON, D.C.

What Is Entomology?

Hi! My name is Dino Martins, and I'm an entomologist.

An entomologist is a scientist who studies insects. Look around outside—insects are everywhere!

locust

I SPEND MOST OF MY TIME OUTSIDE LOOKING AT INSECTS.

I've always loved insects. As a child, I used to sit in the forest and watch them. Some crawled and some flew. My favorite were the butterflies that fluttered down to sip nectar from flowers.

You've probably seen insects before, but have you really looked at them? Observe an insect for five minutes, and soon you'll be asking questions you may never have thought of before. When you see a bee moving slowly on a flower, you'll start to wonder what it's doing.

An entomologist is curious and creative. Although it's an exciting job, it's not always easy. It takes patience to watch quietly and wait for insects to arrive.

Are you creative, patient, curious, and careful? Let's jump into the lives of insects!

A BUTTERFLY SIPS NECTAR FROM A FLOWER.

A MAGNIFYING GLASS HELPS US OBSERVE TINY INSECTS.

A LOG IS THE PERFECT PLACE TO SIT AND WAIT FOR INSECTS TO ARRIVE.

5

Why Do Scientists Study Insects?

honeybee

ENTOMOLOGISTS WANT TO LEARN MORE ABOUT HOW INSECTS HELP OUR PLANET AND WHAT WE CAN DO TO PROTECT THEM.

I study insects because there is so much to discover about them. I say they are the "little creatures that make the world go 'round!" This means that insects play a very important role in nature.

I study pollinators. Pollinators are insects that move pollen from one flower to another. They are very important because they help new plants grow.

Many of the foods we eat come from plants. I study these insects because I want to help farmers grow better crops.

DUNG BEETLES ARE IMPORTANT INSECTS. THEY HELP CLEAN UP EARTH.

DID YOU KNOW THAT TOMATO PLANTS ARE POLLINATED BY BUMBLEBEES?

How Does Studying Insects Help People?

Entomologists ask specific questions, then set up investigations to find the answers. When I wanted to help farmers in Kenya grow crops like mango, coffee, and eggplant, I had to find out which insects and which crops would be the best pairs.

TO HELP FARMERS, I OBSERVED THEIR CROPS AND THE INSECTS THAT VISITED.

Here's what my team and I did.

1. We observed. We watched flowers to see which insects visited them. We recorded the insects that came back and wrote the exact time of day we saw each one.

2. We collected information. We counted the insects that came to visit and timed how long they stayed. We also studied their behavior. We used a counter and a timer to keep track of each insect visiting each flower. We wrote down what we saw.

3. We examined our information. We entered our data into a computer. Then we studied the data to look for patterns.

The patterns told us which crops were right for the kinds of pollinators in their area. That way, the farmers could grow more crops, so more insects could come to visit, so more crops could grow!

mangoes

9

Where Do Insects Live?

common milkweed grasshopper

SOME INSECTS LIVE IN HOT, DRY PLACES.

Insects live almost everywhere! They're found from the coldest Arctic tundras to the tallest mountain on Earth. Entomologists might travel to some of the most extreme and remote corners of the world to study insects.

BEES ARE ATTRACTED TO THESE BRIGHT YELLOW FLOWERS.

I get to travel to some of the wildest parts of Africa. The best place for me to find pollinators is in an area with lots of flowers. One of the places I visit most is in Turkana County, in northern Kenya.

Turkana is hot and dry most of the time. But when it does rain, the desert comes to life! Beautiful flowers appear, and lots of insects arrive to feast on nectar and pollen.

Turkana County

KENYA

EUROPE

ASIA

Atlantic Ocean

AFRICA

Kenya

Indian Ocean

SOUTH AMERICA

I DO A LOT OF RESEARCH IN TURKANA.

Turkana in bloom

What Do Insects Eat?

queen butterfly

WHEN I WAS A CHILD, I WATCHED A BUTTERFLY DRINK NECTAR FROM A FLOWER. I KNEW THEN THAT I WANTED TO STUDY INSECTS.

Insects spend a lot of time looking for food! For pollinators, that works out well for them *and* the plants they feed on. When they visit flowers to get food, insects pick up pollen. As they move from flower to flower, they spread the pollen around. Then new plants grow.

Knowing what kind of food an insect eats is helpful when you want to study that type of insect. To find an insect, just look for evidence of it eating. Find a leaf full of holes, and there might be caterpillars nearby!

Part of being an entomologist is spending a lot of time observing. After finding a juicy leaf full of holes or a flower full of nectar, we wait for the right insect to come along. Then we capture it with a net. Capturing the insect helps us study it up close.

SOME INSECTS ARE MEAT-EATERS. PRAYING MANTISES HUNT FOR THEIR PREY. THEY EAT OTHER INSECTS, SUCH AS FLIES AND CRICKETS.

AN INSECT MADE THESE HOLES BY EATING THE LEAF.

How Do Entomologists Study Insects?

When we capture an insect, we put it into a special box to keep it safe. The box is cold inside, which slows down the insect's body. This means the insect will stay still and will be less likely to get hurt.

When the insect has become very still, we use special tweezers to take it out of the box. We are very careful not to hurt it. Now we can study it up close.

ENTOMOLOGISTS KNOW HOW TO CAREFULLY LIFT INSECTS WITH SPECIAL TWEEZERS.

When I study pollinators, I want to know more about how their bodies help them find and collect pollen. A butterfly has a very long tongue. When we capture a butterfly, we measure the length of its tongue. That gives us clues about which flowers it visits. A long tongue means it can reach nectar inside a long flower!

Some bees have pollen baskets on their legs. That's where they store the pollen they collect while visiting flowers. We can take samples of the pollen to find out more about the flowers they visit.

shield bug

DID YOU KNOW THAT BUGS ARE A CERTAIN TYPE OF INSECT? BUGS HAVE PIERCING AND SUCKING MOUTHPARTS.

A BEE CARRIES POLLEN IN THE BASKET ON ITS LEGS.

15

LIKE BUTTERFLIES, MOTHS HAVE LONG TONGUES TO REACH POLLEN.

Entomologists also study the behavior of insects. To do that, we want to see them out in nature. There, we carefully observe them and record what we see.

When making observations, it's important to record facts. That means we need to record the actual things we see—not how we feel or what we hope to see. That can be hard! Sometimes our observations don't match the patterns we expected.

Here's an example.

You might see this insect, a hawk moth, drinking nectar in the evening.

Are all hawk moths busy as the sun sets? Or just one that you happen to see? To find the answer, we need to collect information at many times during the day, over many days. We also need to make sure we get our data at the same times each day. That makes it easier to compare.

If we don't see any insects, we write that down, too. Writing a zero is just as important as writing 100!

Hawk Moth Observations

Week of: June 5–11

Location: My backyard

	Monday	Tuesday	Wednesday
8am	0	0	0
12pm	1	0	0
4pm	2	1	2
8pm	14	16	12

YOU CAN RECORD YOUR OBSERVATIONS IN A CHART LIKE THIS. ACCORDING TO THIS DATA, WHEN ARE HAWK MOTHS MOST ACTIVE?

Can Insects Hurt People?

ENTOMOLOGISTS WEAR LONG SLEEVES AND PANTS TO PROTECT OUR SKIN FROM INSECTS.

Insects need to have ways to defend themselves. After all, there are other animals that might want to eat them. To some insects, a human can look like a big, hungry animal! So entomologists need to be careful.

One way we can protect ourselves is to look *less* like a big, hungry animal. How can we do that? Many insects can see bright colors. When we wear dull colors, like gray and beige, insects have a harder time seeing us.

Insects also get scared easily! So we avoid sudden movements and always give them space. And remember, most insects don't want to hurt you (though some may see you as a tasty snack). As long as you are careful and give them space, insects will mind their own business!

HAT

SHIRT

PANTS

SHOES

How Are Insects Helpful?

One of the most important reasons I study insects is to learn how they affect our lives. Over time, we've learned just how much insects help people.

Insects do a lot of important jobs for humans, just by going about their daily lives. The more we know about insects—where they live, what they eat, and how they behave—the more *they* can help *us*, and *we* can help *them!*

cacao tree

INSECTS POLLINATE FLOWERS. SOME FLOWERS THEN GROW INTO THE FRUITS AND VEGETABLES WE EAT.

1. Insects help food grow.

2. Insects eat pests.

3. Insects clean up the forest floor.

THESE LADYBUGS EAT SMALL PESTS CALLED APHIDS.

SOME INSECTS EAT DEAD LEAVES AND ROTTEN WOOD. THAT HELPS TO MAKE NEW SOIL.

red wood ants

How Do Insects Get Their Names?

If the insect we're studying is new to science, then one of the last steps in studying it is getting to pick its name.

Many insects have a common name, or a name that most people use. But all insects have a scientific name, too. Some insects are named after the place where they were discovered. Others are named for the person who discovered them or for the way they look.

THIS BUMBLEBEE'S SCIENTIFIC NAME IS *BOMBUS*.

A few years ago, my team and I were in Turkana. It had just rained, and the flowers were blooming. It was very hot and sunny, and there were many different types of bees buzzing around.

Suddenly, some orange bees appeared. I knew these were special. After careful observations, I realized that they had not been studied by other scientists!

So I started to study them. I observed their behavior as they visited flowers. I shared my findings with other scientists. I named the bee *turkana*.

THE FIRST THING I NOTICED ABOUT THE ORANGE BEE WAS THAT IT HAS NO STRIPES. I THEN FOUND OUT THAT IT LIVES ALONE, UNDERGROUND, AND NOT IN A HIVE.

Are There More Insects to Discover?

About one million kinds of insects have already been discovered. Entomologists can't agree on how many more are out there. Some think 10 million, others think 30 million, and still others think 100 million!

blue dasher

Colorado potato beetle

tortoise beetle

praying mantis

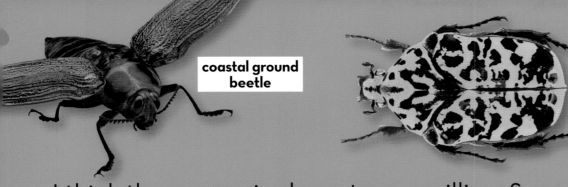
coastal ground beetle

harlequin flower beetle

giant luna moth

I think the answer is closer to 100 million. Some insects can look similar, but they are actually very different. On one farm alone, we were surprised to find about 1,000 different types of pollinators!

That tells me there are many more insects still to be discovered. Imagine you're in the forest and you look around. You might see two or three insects flying or crawling around you. But there are many, many more insects that you *aren't* seeing—and maybe some that *no one* has ever seen.

Maybe you'll be the lucky entomologist who finds them!

hornet

dung beetle

jewel beetle

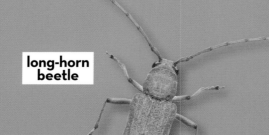
long-horn beetle

Can I Find a New Insect?

Kids make great entomologists!

One time, my team worked with a group of children. They helped us count and record bees. The children set up bee hotels and observed the bees that came and went. Then they sent us their results. Their hard work showed us that different kinds of bees can share a home in the bee hotel. We also learned that different bees build their nests at different times of year.

BEE HOTEL

You can study insects, too.

1. Find a quiet place outside with plants nearby. Wait for interesting insects to visit.

2. Draw a picture of the insects you see. Then count how many different insects you saw. Record your results.

3. Go outside to the same spot at the same time every day for a week. Record what you see. Did the same kinds of insects come by? Did they look the same as the previous ones did? Be sure to draw and count every day.

4. Look at your data! How many insects did you see? What kind did you see most? Look up the insects you saw. Maybe one of them is a brand-new kind!

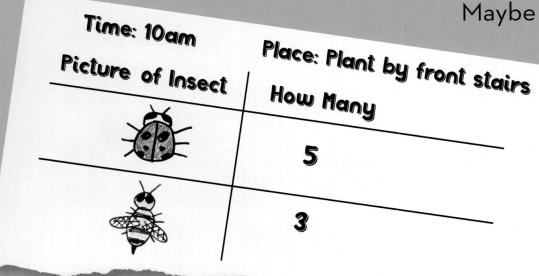

Time: 10am

Place: Plant by front stairs

Picture of Insect	How Many
	5
	3

How Do I Become an Entomologist?

You've learned all about how and why entomologists capture and study insects. There are many ways you can study them, too! You can start by setting up places to observe insects around your home.

Set Up a Pollinator Garden

Ask an adult to help you start up a pollinator garden. You don't need much space—even a balcony or small green patch will do. First, research flowers that grow well in your area and what types of pollinators they attract.

• **Plan where your garden will go.** Observe the area. Record the kinds of plants that are already in the area and the insects you see.

- **Now plant your flowers.** When the flowers bloom, observe again. Are there more insects now?

- **Watch the insects carefully.** How do they get pollen?

Visit museums with insect collections, too. Learn about common insects in your community. Then you can investigate the insects you're interested in to find out more.

I hope you learn to love insects as much as I do. They truly do make the world go 'round! Our planet needs insects!

GLOSSARY

Behavior What someone or something does. For example, some insects land on plants to eat. Others hover in the air near the plant while they eat. Those are different kinds of feeding behaviors.

Collect To gather or add. You can collect things, such as rocks, or you can collect data by making observations and writing them down.

Crop Plants that are used as food for animals or humans. Fruits and vegetables are crops. So are wheat and corn.

Data Information that you have collected. For example, counting the number of insects that visit a certain flower is data. Data is usually measured or counted. Sometimes it's shown as numbers. Other times it's shown in charts or graphs.

Defend To protect. Some insects, like bees, can sting to defend themselves from animals that may try to hurt or eat them.

Entomologist A scientist who studies insects

Evidence Information and observations collected about a specific idea. Evidence can help prove whether or not the idea is true.

Fact Information that's proved to be true

Investigation A planned experiment. An investigation starts with a specific question you'd like to answer and a plan for what evidence you need—and how you'll get it—to answer the question.

Locate To find

Observe To watch carefully, usually to gather data

Pattern A repeating and predictable order of things. For example, a pattern can be that you observe many moths in the evening and not many in the morning over several days.

Pollen Small grains in a flower that help new flowers grow

Pollinator An insect or other animal that helps spread pollen from flower to flower

Record To write down or in other ways keep track of observations

Scientific name The name scientists use to refer to a living thing. Scientific names are usually in Latin.

CREDITS

For Bugs and People Who Love Bugs Everywhere
For all my students, who have been my greatest teachers
For all my teachers, who made me a lifelong student
of the little things that truly run the world!
—DM

Eternally grateful to my family: Joe and Sarah Ellen, Nani and Eric, and my Ma. And those who've helped shape and guide my journey of discovery: N. Pierce, E. O. Wilson, R. Leakey, M. Leakey, S. Miller, P. Kahumbu, G. Boy, C. Ngarachu, E. Whitley, A. Whitley, S. C. Collins, and many others. And for continued support from the Whitley Fund for Nature, Princeton University, and the National Geographic Society. The author and publisher also wish to sincerely thank the book team: Shelby Lees, editor; Shira Evans, text editor; Hilary Andrews, photo editor; Kathryn Robbins, art director and designer; Joan Gossett, production editor; and Anne LeongSon and Gus Tello, design production assistants.

Since 1888, the National Geographic Society has funded more than 12,000 research, exploration, and preservation projects around the world. The Society receives funds from National Geographic Partners, LLC, funded in part by your purchase. A portion of the proceeds from this book supports this vital work. To learn more, visit natgeo.com/info.

NATIONAL GEOGRAPHIC and Yellow Border Design are trademarks of the National Geographic Society, used under license.

For more information, visit nationalgeographic.com, call 1-800-647-5463, or write to the following address:

National Geographic Partners
1145 17th Street N.W.
Washington, D.C. 20036-4688 U.S.A.

Visit us online at nationalgeographic.com/books

For librarians and teachers: ngchildrensbooks.org

More for kids from National Geographic: natgeokids.com

National Geographic Kids magazine inspires children to explore their world with fun yet educational articles on animals, science, nature, and more. Using fresh storytelling and amazing photography, *Nat Geo Kids* shows kids ages 6 to 14 the fascinating truth about the world—and why they should care. kids.nationalgeographic.com/subscribe

For information about special discounts for bulk purchases, please contact National Geographic Books Special Sales: specialsales@natgeo.com

For rights or permissions inquiries, please contact National Geographic Books Subsidiary Rights: bookrights@natgeo.com

Designed by Kathryn Robbins

Hardcover ISBN: 978-1-4263-3354-5
Reinforced library binding ISBN: 978-1-4263-3355-2

Photo Credits:
GI = Getty Images; SS = Shutterstock
Cover, Miroslav Hlavko/SS; (INSET), photo courtesy of Dr. Dino Martins; back cover (LE), anat chant/SS; (RT), photo courtesy of Dr. Dino Martins; front flap, Waravut Wattanapanich/SS; back flap, photo courtesy of Dr. Dino Martins; 1, alslutsky/SS; 2-3, Sean van Tonder/SS; 4, photo courtesy of Dr. Dino Martins; 5 (UP), Doug Lemke/SS; 5 (CTR), Christian Musat/SS; 5 (LO), Hero Images/GI; 6, sumikophoto/SS; 7 (UP), Lisovskaya/GI; 7 (LO LE), Ann & Steve Toon/robertharding/GI; 7 (LO RT), kaanozben/GI; 8, photo courtesy of Dr. Dino Martins; 9 (UP), photo courtesy of Dr. Dino Martins; 9 (CTR LE), justyle/SS; 9 (CTR RT), hanibaram/GI; 9 (LO), Jack Hong/SS; 10 (LE), Fabio Pupin/FLPA/Minden Pictures; 10 (RT), Mitsushi Okada/orion/GI; 11 (UP), NG Maps; 11 (LO LE), Nigel Pavitt/GI; 11 (LO RT), photo courtesy of Dr. Dino Martins; 12, Rolf Nussbaumer/GI; 13 (UP), tenra/GI; 13 (LO), shishir_bansal/GI; 14 (LE), sutichak/GI; 14 (RT), Leonid Eremeychuk/SS; 15 (UP), Radu Bercan/SS; 15 (LO), sumikophoto/SS; 16, Ysign/SS; 17, sittipong/SS; 18, photo courtesy of Dr. Dino Martins; 19 (UP LE), Gyvafoto/SS; 19 (UP RT), Tarzhanova/GI; 19 (CTR), BEAUTYofLIFE/SS; 19 (LO), Jiri Hera/SS; 20, sursad/SS; 21 (UP), Andre Skonieczny/GI; 21 (LO), Emanuel Tanjala/Alamy Stock Photo; 22, Ian Grainger/SS; 23, Cecilia Lewis/Courtesy of Dino Martins; 23, photo courtesy of Dr. Dino Martins; 24 (UP LE), Le Do/SS; 24 (LO LE), Krailurk Warasup/SS; 24 (LO CTR), Vitalii Hulai/SS; 24 (LO RT), Ziva_K/GI; 25 (UP LE), Image Ideas; 25 (UP CTR), Cosmin Manci/SS; 25 (UP RT), Michael G Smith/SS; 25 (CTR RT), akiyoko/SS; 25 (LO LE), tea maeklong/SS; 25 (LO CTR), Protasov AN/SS; 25 (LO RT), Photobee/Dreamstime; 26, fotomem/GI; 27, Hilary Andrews/NG Staff; 28, GH Photos/Alamy Stock Photo; 29 (UP), Michael H/GI; 29 (LO), photo courtesy of Dr. Dino Martins; 32 (UP), photo courtesy of Dr. Dino Martins; 32 (LO LE), Miroslav Hlavko/SS; 32 (LO CTR), alslutsky/SS; 32 (LO RT), Sean van Tonder/SS

Printed in China
18/PPS/1

cover: blue damselfly

page 1: dead-nettle leaf beetle

pages 2–3: elegant grasshopper